WORLDS

POETRY & PROSE

OF

BEAU TAPLIN

YOU

Andrews McMeel
PUBLISHING®

Andrews McMeel Publishing
a division of Andrews McMeel Universal
1130 Walnut Street, Kansas City, Missouri 64106

www.andrewsmcmeel.com

18 19 20 21 22 BVG 10 9 8 7 6 5 4 3 2 1

ISBN: 978-1-4494-9549-7

Library of Congress Control Number: 2018933438

Cover design by Lucy Jane Brand @lucyjanebrand
Cover images: photography by Bella Kotak, bellakotak.com © 2017
Internal design and typesetting by Lucy Jane Brand @lucyjanebrand
Illustrations copyright © Anita Maslov 2017; all other internal images:
shutterstock.com

ATTENTION: SCHOOLS AND BUSINESSES
Andrews McMeel books are available at quantity discounts with bulk purchase for educational, business, or sales promotional use. For information, please e-mail the Andrews McMeel Publishing Special Sales Department: specialsales@amuniversal.com.

To all who believe in the splendor
of stars and the miracle of being alive.

Also by Beau Taplin

Bloom

Introduction

In collecting the pieces together for *Worlds of You*, I have found myself reflecting on my reasons for writing, and the reasons we all gravitate toward art as a way of better understanding and healing our pain. When I was nine, I lost my grandmother to lung cancer. It was my first encounter with loss, and the sharp pain of her passing was like nothing I had felt before. My grandmother and I had always shared a close bond. A woman of contrasts, she would work the paddocks of her country home dressed in precious white-gold jewelry and a pair of hot-pink gum boots, and while her tongue could be sharp at times, when you needed her, there was no one so loving and warm.

I can remember the funeral well. During the ceremony, a cousin of mine stood up to sing a rendition of the Celine Dion song "Call the Man." Her performance took the breath of everyone in the room, and when she stepped down from the stage, I immediately noticed a striking change in the expressions of all around me. Where before there had been only sorrow, a tender lightness took its place. The room erupted in applause and shared a small moment of joy, and it was then I first recognized the power of art. Through the words of a simple song, my cousin had moved us all and honored my grandmother's life with her voice. She had reshaped our pain into something hopeful and bright.

That night, I returned home with a heavy heart, but inspired to celebrate my grandmother in my own way. With neither the talent nor the confidence to stand up and sing, my quiet, timid nine-year-old self chose instead to write a short poem in her memory. Thankfully, no one ever threw it out.

Nan

Nan is sweet,
Nan is nice,
always giving good advice.
When I was sad,
she wouldn't nag,
instead she
made me better.

I suppose these were the first words I ever wrote from the heart. They were humble beginnings, of course, endearingly simple and wrought with misspellings, and I wouldn't write creatively again for another fifteen years, but I have come to regard this moment in my life as significant. From then on, art became my way of exploring both the difficult and beautiful things in life. When I felt like an outcast at school, I painted and I drew. When my heart was captured or broken, I would stay up long nights writing music. And then at twenty-four, at my lowest point, I started writing again, and so my creative journey came full circle. But no matter the medium, the purpose was always the same; creative expression was a coping mechanism for me, a way of better understanding the mysteries of myself and the world around me.

What I have come to believe is that all art is a window, and through this window we enter worlds where light and dark embrace and dance together. They are places where we can feel fearless in our emotions because they show us we are never alone in them.We look at a painting and find ourselves in the brushstrokes.We listen to a piece of music and it is like our hearts composed the melody. We read the words and collapse to our knees with the poet. We roar with the thunder. We burn with the stars.

Worlds of You is a collection of my most treasured works dating all the way back to the beginning of my journey. Divided into two parts, the first, "Heart," represented by the rose, brings together pieces inspired by the loves I have known in my life and the lessons I have drawn from them. My primary hope in sharing them with you now is to show that we all experience feelings of passion, powerlessness, confusion, and loss, and they are not something we should ever attempt to escape or avoid. Love is supposed to have sharp edges, it is supposed to be messy and unsensible, and if you go your whole life trying to keep your heart out of harm's way, you miss out on all of love's magic.

The second, "Spirit," symbolized by the violet, collects together a series of works that concentrate on the self. I have always believed self-understanding to be the most meaningful journey we take in our lives, and by the time you are finished reading through these pages, my hope is that you feel encouraged to look at yourself more closely, to explore who you are and what gives you life.

If nothing else, the message I hope you draw from this collection is that we all experience suffering and we all experience joy, but when you live in open conversation with your heart, life— in its completeness—becomes beautiful, even the very dark times.

Beau Taplin

HEART

Worlds in You

There are
     worlds in you,

and I have
     fallen in love
     with every one.

The Awful Truth

One day, whether you
are 14,
28,
or 65

you will stumble upon
someone who will start
a fire in you that cannot die.

However, the saddest,
most awful truth
you will ever come to find,
is they are not always
with whom we spend our lives.

Love's Simple Pleasures

You remind me
so much of life's simple pleasures
and everything effortless
and sweet in the world.
      A good read.
            Fresh, clean sheets.
                  A quick dip in the sea.
      A cozy, rainy Sunday morning
with a hot cup of coffee
and no place to be.

The Intellect

The secret is to find someone who engages you deeply, to form a connection that goes further than desire or lust. It's not enough to covet only a face or a body; true chemistry begins with the intellect and heart.

Free Will

Perhaps there were no soul mates, I thought, and love was neither written in the stars nor planned by the gods but a choice, one built of hope and sweat and blood and trust.

Not served up on a silver platter by a whim of fate but something that must be earned and fought for.

Astronomy

You want to know what it was? The moment I
knew you were it? It was when I showed you the
darkest parts of me, and instead of running away,
you rolled out a blanket, lay on your back, and
pointed out the stars.

Hello Goodbye

Goodbyes take a great deal of courage, but what
takes even more is the hello that comes next.
To cast your aversions aside despite all you have
suffered and take a chance on somebody new.
To risk it all again because you see that human
connection is precious and rare and always
worth the risk.

I gave you
a second chance.
I ran back into
a burning house
to save the
things I loved.

Into My Arms

I want to be the one
whose arms you run
to whether you have
reason to rejoice or
cause to collapse.

Don't Pity Me

Don't pity me.
I am not in love with you
because I want to be.
You are in my veins
like a disease.
The memory of you
is corrosive.
Acidic.
And I am bent
day and night
on looking for a cure
just to rid myself of it.

In Tune

There's something unusual about us.
Something deeply spiritual.
The way we fall into one another
so naturally like our love
was carved of the earth.
There are star systems
bursting at our fingertips
when we touch.
We are in tune.
Our hearts croon the same old song.
The universe planned for us.
I know it. I know it.

Stay

Stay. I know it's probably the wrong thing to do.
You and I have gone dark. We are dead in the water.
And all we seem to do anymore is dream up new
ways to hurt each other. Look, I'm under no illusions.
I know this is the end of the line for us. The damage
has been done. We have fallen too far. But for a few
more moments, do you think we could just forget
all that? Do you think we could dim the lights a
little and just lie here together? We have the rest
of our lives to go our separate ways, misplace
each other's names, and become strangers again.
Stay here for tonight. Let's be messy and careless.
Tomorrow is another day, let's worry about it then.
Curl up into our love. Hit pause on this awfulness.
Stay, won't you? Just awhile longer.

Chalkboards

The thought of you
is ever present.
Some days, it is faint and small,
like a whisper in the dark,
and others, unbearable,
like nails screeching
down a chalkboard.
But, whatever the case,
you are always on my mind.

Every day,
        every hour,
                every minute.

The Moment

You always had this little way
of making the dull and dreary
bright and radiant,
        the ordinary
                extraordinary,
                        the mundane magic.

To you, everything was an adventure.
And in your silly, wild presence,
I always felt like every
moment mattered,
that all of life should be
embraced and cherished.

Life Stories

Everyone you meet has a part to play in
your story. And while some may take a chapter,
others a paragraph, and most will be no more
than scribbled notes in the margins, someday
you'll meet someone who will become so integral
to your life, you'll put their name in the title.

Memory Deleted

The sorry thing about loss is it's not the pain
that beats me but the fear the pain will pass.
That sooner or later I will pull myself together
and move on. That's the killing blow. To know
that someday, no matter how hard I fight it,
I will forget how it felt to love you.

Real Loss

They say you don't know what you've got till it's
gone, but fact is, with you I always did. Not a day
went by I didn't thank the stars or worship the
earth you walked on. That is real loss. To know
what you have, to cherish every moment, and
then watch it slip away.

Truth

When it comes to relationships, I have only one rule: give me truth, however cold or cruel or hard it is to hear.

I would rather have my heart broken, if it means I can then release the hurt and move on, than waste a single moment of my time being fooled by a lie intended to preserve my feelings.

A Most Unwise Thing

There may come a time in your life when the universe will ask you to do something fantastically foolish for the person you love.

I pray that you rise to this challenge with daring and grace. That you always recognize the wisdom in risking anything and everything for the good of your heart.

The Greatest Weight

And in that moment
I swore
that nothing
in this universe
could be so heavy
as the absence
of the person you love.

Wild Ocean

She was the tide,
always drifting
     in
and
     out
of the lives of those
who loved her,
eternally indecisive,
unable to discern
whether she desired
the solidity and safety
of land,
or the wild freedom
of the ocean.

Quality Time

The quality of a friendship should be measured on the strength of your bond and the abundance of love between you, not the number of times you catch up over coffee or go out drinking.

We all have different needs, schedules, and responsibilities. What's important is you are there when it matters.

The Best in Me

You bring out the best in me. I don't mean better manners, or a sense of maturity, or whatever else this tired world expects of me.

I mean you make me want to climb roofs, run wild and act inappropriately, take risks and pursue my dreams with passion and integrity. Around you, I start living.

Fallback

My heart does not
      have a fallback,
      no plan B
      or fail-safe,

it's you
or no one else.

Her soul
was utterly
captivating.
A warm rainy
day dying to be
danced in.

The Wrong Call

That's what's so damn difficult
    about making the decision to leave.
Whether it's the right or wrong call
    the hurt's just the same.

One Fraction of a Moment

It is a frightening thought,
        that in one fraction of a moment
you can fall in the kind of love
        that takes a lifetime to get over.

The Important Things

A meaningful and passionate romance isn't all about grand, extravagant gestures. In the end, it is not the restaurants, the getaways, or expensive gifts that are hardest to release and forget but the in-jokes, the long talks, your understanding of each other. The things you cannot replace.

Act Cool

I don't do detached. I won't play hard to get or act cool for the sake of appearing elusive. If I like you, I'm all in. If you have my attention, then it's because I genuinely care for you. But betray my trust, and without even thinking twice, I will burn that bridge and never look back.

Sixth Sense

A friend was someone with a sixth sense, someone
who could read the silences between your words and
knew precisely how hard to push when you were on
the verge of a poor decision, someone who showed
up with a bottle of wine and a shoulder to lean on
before you even knew that was what you needed.

The Chance Meeting

It hurts my head to think of how many things had
to happen for our paths to intersect. Of all those
numberless little fortunes that led me to you.
A broken alarm clock, a delayed train, a sudden
downpour, and there we were. You and I, sharing
coffee, our whole lives ahead of us.

Little Burning Lights

We sit in silence and watch the stars. I suppose
because there are no words, not in all the languages
on earth, that can properly describe the feeling of
being in love, and perhaps those little burning lights
out there in the dark are the closest we come to
something that does.

The Test

Goodbyes are important. They are how we know
we are doing the right thing. If they come easy,
then by all means leave and never look back.
But if you open your mouth and feel the words
get stuck like glue in your throat, you are making
a terrible mistake.

Distance

You don't know distance
    until you've shared your bed
with someone who's falling
    out of love with you.

The Echo

I like to think that loneliness
        is just the echo of missing a person
you haven't had the pleasure
        of meeting quite yet.

Light & Noise

A funny thing happens when you miss someone badly enough. I can be in a room full of friendly faces, surrounded by laughter and celebration, but to me it is just light and noise. I will smile and make small talk, but it is all a performance. The truth is, I am someplace else with you.

With Dignity

Once someone has let you go emotionally, it's over,
no matter how tightly or desperately you commit
to hang on.

    Better to release yourself from the relationship
with your dignity intact than fight a losing battle
and risk lasting damage to your heart.

Professionals

Perhaps the two of us
had become so good at leaving

once we had found something
worth keeping

we did not know
how to stay.

I want you,
desperately,
whether we are
a match made
in heaven or a
beautiful disaster
just waiting
to happen.

Stay Friends

I used to believe that the only sensible way to cope
with the end of a love was to sever ties and move on.
But I see now that true connection is rare, and to be
understood by somebody is much too precious a
thing to lose. So, however hard or much it hurts,
I am standing by you.

A Healthy Relationship

Listen, a healthy relationship isn't living vicariously through one another. True love isn't someone being there at your side every moment of every day but feeling free and encouraged to pursue your own passions and then sharing in the spoils of your triumphs together.

Forgiveness

I forgive you, not for you but for me.
Because, like chains
shackling me to the past,
I will no longer pollute
my heart with bitterness,
fear, distrust, or anger.
I forgive you because hate
is just another way of holding on,
and you don't belong here anymore.

My Demons

You deserve everything there is to give.
Breakfasts in bed.
Diamonds on your doorstep.
Little notes hidden everywhere.
I want you to have all of my secrets
and all of my demons,
because you especially deserve
all the parts of me
I'm usually too afraid to share.

And You

There are a few things in life
so beautiful they hurt:
swimming in the ocean while it rains,
reading in empty libraries,
the sea of stars that appears
when you are miles away from the city,
bars after 2am,
a bed of roses in bloom,
all the things we do not yet know
about the universe, and you.

The Promise 1

A soul mate is a meeting of mind, spirit, and body
with someone whose strengths, flaws, and energy
perfectly complement your own. It is steady ground,
a shelter in a storm, a point on a map when you are
wayward and lost. The promise of a place to come
home to for as long as you are here in the world.

Good Morning

I want to begin the rest of my days with strong cups of coffee and the sight of your lashes fluttering open, ignoring alarms and sharing showers, discussing our plans and aspirations, and wishing each other a pleasant day knowing, with beginnings as sweet and simple as these, it can only get better.

Illogical Tendency

I have an illogical tendency to only desire the things that are difficult. It does not matter how kind or committed a person might be, if they come easily, I'll quickly grow uninterested. But threaten my heart, safety, or sanity, and I'm all yours.

True Intimacy

True intimacy is more than fooling around with somebody you are physically attracted to. I want to share myself with someone who will press her hands through the surface of my skin, curl herself up inside my soul and say, *"Here, this is who I am."*

Long Distance

When they work, long-distance relationships are the best sort of beautiful, I think. That a person could wait months, cross miles and oceans for a few short spectacular moments with the person they love, that's it, you know, that's what we're all searching for.

A Prayer

I hope to God
        I feel again

what I have felt
        for you.

All of us are
looking for
some kind
of escape.
Occasionally,
we find it
in each other.

Phobia

What am I
most afraid of?

That maybe
you were it
and I
let you go.

Three Things

I learned the people
    we love usually
    turn out
to be one of three things:
    a home,
        a holiday,
            or hell.

The Pressure

What a sad thought it is
that some of us
will surrender
and settle down
long before
we have met the person
we are supposed to love.

Awfully Beautiful

I find the single most remarkable thing about love is the way it is doomed to pain and loss from its onset. Whether it is the spouse that outlives their lover, or loses them to another, there is no escaping this most solemn of inevitabilities.

That two people would commit themselves to all of this hurt and heartache in spite of this, all in the name of experiencing genuine connection for even a moment, is the proof I need that madness exists, and it is awfully beautiful.

You Deserve Better

And I learned
"You deserve better"

was sometimes no more
than a synonym for

*"I don't want to hurt you,
and I want you to be happy,*

*but I don't love you
anymore."*

The Way

You get me.
There's no other way to put it.
When I am a whirlwind of a person,
a mess of bad moods
and even worse ideas,
you move in slowly,
wrap each of those arms around me,
and in an instant,
I feel understood.
When I am blind of all else,
I see the way through you.

Ticking Clock

Sure, things didn't work out
the way I had hoped.
Maybe I thought we'd get married,
have a couple of kids,
build ourselves a little house
with a fireplace in the hills.
But then,
what does that really matter?
You are the love of my life.
I never needed us
to last a lifetime to know that.

The Great Floods

Oh darling, do not be ashamed of the way you
cry for him. It does not give him power over you.

Like the great floods of old you are simply
washing yourself of wickedness, and soon he will
be forgotten.

Come Over

Come over. I don't really mind whether we talk for hours, get blind drunk, or sit together in silence and look up at the stars. Sometimes the world down here just gets a bit much, and I need to lose myself in someone's company for a little while.

The Slow Death

I sense that I am slowly letting go. That I'm growing less in love with you every single day.

I think that's the most difficult thing about losing someone you have loved: the way you feel never really dies at once. All you can do is wait and watch it turn back to dust, one day at a time.

I *plant roots so
deeply in the people
I love that I always
lose a piece of myself
when they go.*

The Final Piece

Don't wait around your whole life for somebody
who completes you. That's not how it works.
You are the sum total of everybody you have
ever lusted for and loved.

Drink life in through your lips, dig your nails
into its skin, undress and kiss the neck of it before
you settle down. A soul mate is not the whole picture,
remember that; they are just the final piece.

The Measurement

A relationship should not be measured in months
or years. It's the caliber of the memories that matter.
Their impact, their permanence, and the degree to
which they change you.

I've had relationships lasting years I can now
scarcely recollect, and hours with others that feel
like infinities.

Nostalgia

It is a dangerous thing to romanticize the past.
To allow nostalgia to drag up old memories from
the depths of our hearts and fashion them into
something they're not.

We built a mirage from a memory and knelt
before it like a false god. What we called love was
nothing but foolish hope.

A Careful Compromise

Yes, love is all about sacrifice and compromise,
but it's important also to establish a limit.
You shouldn't have to throw your whole life
away to make a relationship work.

If you have to lose yourself to please your
partner, you're with the wrong person.

The Falling

The rains have their oceans
  and the sun has its moon.

Everything needs
  a reason for falling

  and I have you.

Close Enough

It was never love,

but we carried
the same scars,

and sometimes
that is close enough.

Journal Entries

*"I am simply thankful
for your existence,"*

I wrote.

Whether I am meant
to be a part of it or not.

Illuminate

There's no more precious a privilege than to be loved without reserve or judgment. To look deeply into your partner's eyes and see that, despite your many faults and flaws, you are cherished precisely as you are. Once you have known a love like that in your life, it stays with you forever.

The Promise 2

You're important to me. I think if there's anything that will last forever, it's that. Whether we separate, stay in touch, or rarely speak again, you will always be that little someone I really do care for, that I would sacrifice everything for, to protect and keep safe.

Relentless

The way I love you is relentless. It breaks my
concentration when I am busy and drifts my mind
away to thoughts of you when I am in the middle
of conversation. Like a desperate, needy child, it
pokes and prods tirelessly for my attention.
And in the end, it always gets it.

Seven Billion People

The terrifying thing about love is its power to make
an earth populated by over seven billion people
feel like it is inhabited by only one. Making our own
little worlds heaven if they're here, and a lonely hell
if they're not.

One Certainty

If the person you love
makes you question
over and over
if you are enough,
only one thing is certain:
they aren't.

Empty Spaces

I am tired of trying
to fill up my empty spaces

with things I don't need
and people I don't love.

Unpredictable

It terrifies me how talented
you are at turning
your emotions
     on
        and
          off.

How you can be so kind and loving
one moment
then cold like ice the next.

When you open your mouth,
I never know whether
it's going to be
     "I *love you*,"
        or "It's *over*."

Lovely, Dark Things

I don't know what it is,
but you do things to me,

lovely, dark things.

Even
the gentle, unexpected
graze of your hand on mine is
annihilating.

Ultimately,
the worst kinds
of pain do not
come from your
enemies but
the people you
trust and love.

A Sacred Love

Somebody who betters you. Somebody who inspires and encourages you in love and in life, who pushes you toward dreams and goals you'd otherwise ignore, who selflessly sacrifices their time to helping you become a more courageous, well-rounded, and happy human being. That is sacred. You hold on to a love like that.

The Argument

I am not afraid of an argument. Get emotional. Get angry. Spit language venom. Be fierce and unrelenting with your words, if you feel you have to be.

Because, above all else, I am terrified of the silence, of things becoming so passionless between us there is no longer anything left worth fighting for.

Unpreventable

Once a deep and powerful connection between two people has been made they become a vital part of each other's lives and there is no separating them. No measure of distance or duration of silence can prevent the outbreak of smiles and laughter or the strong desire to leap into each other's arms when they come together once more.

Broken Love

There is nothing so beautifully sincere as a brokenhearted person's love. For in giving it they are saying, *"Yes, I have burned to smoke and ash for the ones I have loved. I have been devoured, slowly, then spat back out. And probability suggests you are likely to ruin me too. But here, have my heart. Take it. I'd like you to."*

My Wandering Mind

I don't care if what we have
will never be love.
If we weren't together
in a past life
or written in the stars.
All you need to know
is that when my mind
wanders off
it is always home to you.

Belly Laugh

What do I love most about you?
You make me laugh.
God, you make me laugh.

And I don't mean a little chuckle
 or titter
  or giggle
   or snort.

I mean the kind of laugh
 that howls
  and trembles
   and puts tears in my eyes.

The kind that booms and bellows
 and spreads like wildfire.

The kind I can feel in my soul.

The Liberation

Why should a relationship mean settling down?
Wait for someone who won't let life escape
you, who'll challenge you and drive you toward
your dreams. Someone spontaneous you can get
lost in the world with. A relationship with the
right person is a release, not a restriction.

The Connection

My heart is not captured easily. I am uninterested in small talk, disillusioned by love, and too focused on my dreams and aspirations to lend anybody my attention for long. But if we make that connection, if you find your way into my heart, I will fall for you like gravity has let go of the earth.

Fools Together

I know we needed some time apart,
a little space to reevaluate
what we're looking for,
and should we ever find
our way back to each other
I know we'll be better for it.
Still, I miss you.
And most of the time
I think it would be better
to be fools together
than sensible without you.

The Defining Moment

You were an unexpected surprise.
The defining moment.
The collision of stars
that slammed into me hard
and sent my neat little world
plummeting into the ocean.
I never expected it to be you,
you know?
But it is you.
It's all you.
And now there's no looking back.

Skin Cells

Scientific fact:
our skin cells replace
themselves entirely
once every
two to four weeks,
while the collection of cells
that make up the heart
can take upward
of twenty years.
This is why the body
forgets a person's touch,
long before it forgets
how to love them.

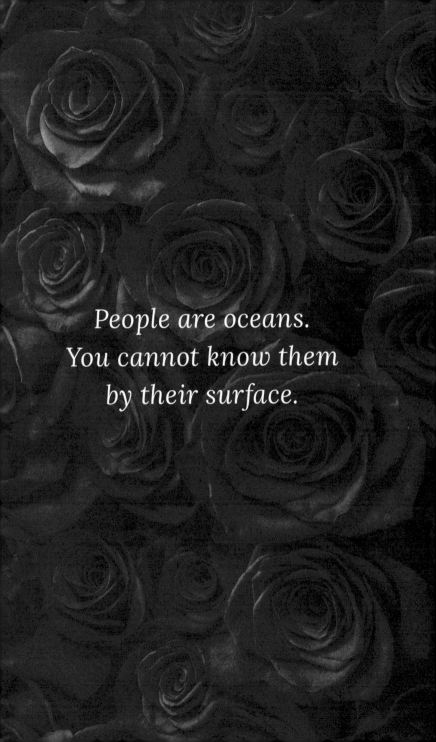

People are oceans.
You cannot know them
by their surface.

Hostels & Homes

By all means, go out into the world and explore with
your heart. Fall in and out of love until your hands
are libraries of all the people they have touched.
Before long, we all learn, right down to our bones,
that some people are hostels and others are homes.

Some Things

I came to realize that there were some things in life you would never get over, some transgressions you could not forget or forgive yourself for, some pains that would not pass, some people you would never stop missing.

The Long Road

It's been a long, hard road, but I've finally found the
closure I need to move on. I've learned to accept
that my all is not always going to be enough and love
is neither owed nor earned; it either is or it's not.
I gave you the world, but you wanted the stars.

The Softest Blue

I know you're not supposed to look to other people
to save you, but whenever I'm around you the world
becomes simple. My moods lift and the skies shift
from smoke and smog to the softest blue. I know
I'm meant to save myself, but the fact is, with you
I don't have to.

The Ego

I'm not looking for somebody who will whisper sweet nothings into my ear to feed the ravenous ego of my heart. But someone who can look me straight in the eye and say, "*I love you, whether you fail or fall, just as you are.*"

Separate Journeys

Timing is a hell of a thing. In the end, that's all it comes down to. The potency of an attraction or the purity of a connection means very little if you are on separate journeys. You and I were a perfect fit. We were. There was just too much distance between us to see it.

Senselessly

I love senselessly or not at all.

I cannot give myself away
to those who do not consume me,
no matter how kind
or committed they are,
but capture the full attention
of my heart,
and however toxic
you are for me,
I would conquer the world
in your name if you asked.

The Fictions of People

Often, when we have a crush, when we lust for
a person, we see only a small percentage of who
they really are. The rest we make up for ourselves.
Rather than listen, or learn, we smother them
in who we imagine them to be, what we desire
for ourselves. We create little fantasies of people
and let them grow in our hearts. And this is
where the relationship fails.

In time, the fictions we've created will fall
away, the lies we tell ourselves quickly unravel,
until soon the person standing in front of you
is almost unrecognizable. You are now complete
strangers in your own love. And what a terrible
shame it is. My advice: pay attention to the small
details of people. You will learn that the universe
is far more spectacular an author than we could
ever hope to be.

The Declaration

This is me, here, hands out, heart open. I want all of you and then some. Your 2am lows and all of your brokenness. To know what terrifies you most so I can tear it to pieces. To explore all of the mysteries of your infinite heart. To show you the way all of your shortcomings and flaws, those small, human imperfections that separate us from the gods, are the very things about you that I will always fall for the hardest.

Bewilder Me

Bewilder me. That's what I'm looking for.
With every passing year I've grown exceedingly
weary and complacent. Nothing interests
me anymore.

I want to be kissed clueless. I want my
attention to be gripped for more than a few
moments. I want to be stunned and surprised
and compelled to second-guess every damn
thing I think I know about the universe.

Hell Exists

Hell exists.
It's here.
3am
awake and
without you.

You remind me
of what my heart
is capable of.
Such terrible,
lovely things.

Homesick

He kissed
her cheek

and then
she knew

that you could
become homesick
for people too.

Too Wrong

We don't mean
to hurt each other,
but we do.
And perhaps
no matter how
right we are
for each other,
we'll always be a little
too wrong.

Growing Pains

Painfully, we all learn
very early on
that a human being
can break you
in a few short, simple words.

Anywhere, Anytime

Falling for a person isn't a process.
You can't plan for it in advance
or anticipate its arrival.
Love strikes in single moments.
Anywhere, anytime.
One day you catch a glimpse of them
gardening in the sun
or singing tunelessly in the shower,
and you think to yourself,
"Oh, I could spend all my life with you."

Decisions

But there is good and bad
in anything.

And at the end of the day,
all we have to decide

is who we share
that good and bad with.

Déjà Vu

You felt familiar the moment I met you.
A lovely sort of déjà vu.
When we spoke or laughed or danced
I became overwhelmed
by the powerful sensation
that I had been here before.
And when we kissed
I felt the energies
of a thousand lives on our lips,
like our souls
had known each other all along.

Little Pieces

I am little pieces
of everyone
I have met,
but I cherish most
the parts
that were yours.

A Fool's Truth

I think I keep telling myself
you never loved me at all
because it is far less terrifying
a prospect than the possibility
you did, you really, truly
did, but all of a sudden, and for
no particular reason,
you woke up one day and stopped.

Kiss me
mercilessly.
Leave no corner
untouched.

Half-Remembered Dream

It's a strange thing to see you now and be unable
to recall how it felt to love you. Like a half-
remembered dream, the essence of what we
shared is there, but the details are all hazy.
Like the house I grew up in, you're still familiar
to me, but the feeling of home is now missing.

The Slow Dance

A recent scientific study found that the hearts of lovers really do beat in sync—that after only a few moments of close proximity they will begin to follow each other's lead until they beat as one. As though our very hearts leap out of our chests and ask one another to dance.

Half Measures

There are no
half measures in love.
Only all or nothing.
And if it doesn't make you
tremble or go mad
at the very thought
of its absence,
you should quietly let go
and move on.

Love, Fear & Hesitation

Sadly, too many of us stay together
    far longer than we should

because it's easier to say, "I *love you*,"
    than it is to say, "I *don't*."

Vacancies

There's a big part of me
    that wishes I never met you.

I preferred the emptiness in me
    when I didn't know it was there.

The Raw End

Do not feel sorry for me.
I mean, who really got
the raw end
of the deal here?

I only lost you,
a lying, frightened,
using, and abusive
poor excuse
for a human being.

And you lost me.

The Explorers

Home is not where
you are from,

it is where
you belong.

Some of us
travel the whole
world to find it.

Others
find it in a person.

The Problem

The problem was
    I wanted to be yours
more than I ever
    wanted to be mine.

In pieces
or perfectly
together,
I adore you
just the
same.

The Arsenal

I have learned that people
will stay, leave, save,
and destroy you,
but by far
the most dangerous thing
they can ever do
is come back.

Damn the Stars

I know we can't seem to catch
a break. And sometimes it feels like
the whole universe is conspiring
against us. But damn the stars, I
choose you. And whatever the odds,
no challenge or obstacle will ever
be enough to stand in our way.

Telescopes

I look to her in the simplest, smallest moments—
when she reads or drinks coffee or brushes her
teeth—and I am breathless, knowing it does not
take a million-dollar telescope to witness the
crushing beauty of the universe.

Eternal Matter

There are those you will love until the end.
Certain feelings are too powerful to perish, and
they quietly survive on in the heart for life.

No matter how much we change or drift
apart, in some small way you will always be mine,
and I will always be yours.

Priorities

I want somebody with a sharp intellect and a heart from hell. Somebody with eyes like star fire and a mouth with a kiss like a bottomless well. But mostly I just want somebody who knows how to love me when I do not know how to love myself.

A Positive Impact

The most important thing you can do for your partner is encourage and inspire meaningful growth. Take every opportunity to contribute to the lives and progress of those you love. A sincere and positive impact will last a lifetime, even if the relationship does not.

The Rehearsal

If it hurts more than it
makes you happy,
then take the lesson
and leave.
Listen,
it is going to be okay.
Some people are only
rehearsals for the real thing.

Small, Quiet Gestures

Some show love rarely
and mostly in small, quiet gestures;
sharing an umbrella in the rain,
leaving you the last slice of pizza,
throwing their arms around you when
you're feeling upset or afraid.
Love does not have to be flamboyant
or loud to be present.

The Goodnight

I want to fall to sleep with you, and I couldn't care
less whether it is in layer upon layer of clothing
or only our skin. All I really want is to wake up not
knowing where I end and you begin.

Moon Landing

It is incredible how alone one person's absence can make you feel. I could be in a room surrounded by all my friends and family, but without you I might as well be standing on the surface of the moon.

The Corner

There's a corner of my heart that is yours. And I don't mean for now, or until I've found somebody else. I mean forever. I mean to say that whether I fall in love a thousand times over or never again, there'll always be a small, quiet place in my heart that belongs only to you.

I never
wanted a
quiet, sensible
sort of love.
I wanted to be
devoured.

The Patient Heart

Settle your heart, child,
your time will come.
One of these days
you will meet eyes
with someone
who makes you feel
so at home in the world
you will think to yourself,
"Ah, *there you are*."

Mistrust

How can I trust in love?
How can I trust
in anything
that can be so present
one moment
and so absent the next?

A Simple Calculation

The more time
and distance
you put
between us,
the larger
you grow in my heart.

Unexpected Goodbye

Whoever said actions
speak louder than words

has never been silenced
by the deafening howl

of a small, unexpected goodbye.

The Hostage

If you're with her and you wish you were elsewhere, then leave. One of the cruelest things you can do to a person is make them feel like home when, to you, they're only temporary. We all deserve adoration and undistracted attention. We all deserve to feel complete. If you can't give her your whole heart, then don't you dare hold hers hostage.

The Stars Will Sigh

And I still hold on to this small, childish hope that there is someone out there in this mad, wild world so completely, utterly meant for me that even the stars will sigh, "At *last!*" in relief at our meeting.

Lovesick

The fact that the word *lovesick* exists, that the simple absence of a person can make you feel physically ill, says a great deal about the terrible power of the human heart.

The Sea Storm

There was something tremendously powerful
about her. Like the sea, it never mattered whether
she was still and serene or in the throes of a storm,
there was always a danger of drowning.

The Last

You might not be the first to crawl into my heart,
kiss me apart, or share my skin in the dark, but you
could be the first one who matters; you could be
the first one who lasts.

The Power of People

That is the power of people,
I suppose;

every other little thing in your life
could be going perfectly to plan,

but if you are missing somebody,
it's hell.

Perfecting the Art

It's you. It's been you
        for as long as I can remember.

Everyone else has been
        just another failed attempt

at perfecting the art
        of pretending you're not.

Storage Box

Be careful.
There are people
out there who will
look at your love
only as a place
to put their pain.

The Privilege

It was a privilege
to love you,
and it was a privilege
to let you go.
Both helped shape me
into the person
I have become.

A Reminder

And you said,
"Never forget me,"

as if the coast
could forget the ocean

or the lung
could forget the breath

or the earth
could forget the sun.

The Leap & the Fall

"I trusted him. I gave him everything.
And still, he left."

"But that's the risk you take.
It's not his fault, child.
That's life.
That's love.

"They call it falling in love
because sometimes you're caught,
and sometimes you're not."

Welcome Home

It is so simple
and effortless with you.
Every moment
sounds like *"Welcome home."*

It's sad, isn't it?
I once thought
worlds of you and
now you're just
another lesson.

Divine Intervention

You're a miracle,
    I still believe that.
You just happened
    to someone else.

My Greatest Sorrow

But above all else,
I wish
for your happiness,
even should you
require
my absence to find it.

The BAC of Forgetting

You can drink too much
and forget the night before,
but I've learned you
can never drink enough
to forget the people
you've loved and lost.

Lifetimes Ago

I knew right away
that you were it for me,

there were
no reservations
or second thoughts,

I saw you
and in an instant
knew in my bones,

my soul
had known your soul
lifetimes ago.

Goodbye

Goodbye,
that cruel, forsaken word,
how smoothly
it forms in the mouth,
how lightly
it falls off the tongue,
how violently
it dismantles a heart.

Imperfect

Do not call me perfect.
A lie is never
a compliment.
Call me an erratic,
damaged,
and insecure mess.
Then tell me that you
love me for it.

Moon Phases

But how can you love a person who is not whole?
Because you, like the moon, are not only beautiful
when full. In all of your phases and fractions and
ivory-white pieces, I love you.

The World Keeps on Spinning

They promise me the world will keep on spinning
without you, but honestly, that is what worries
me most.

The Blood Pact

I am not perfect. I am sometimes selfish, occasionally self-destructive, and prone to very brief, yet severe, spells of sadness. But I would fight until every bone in my body was broken to protect you. That's a promise.

Translations

I'm now fairly certain that the small crack in your voice right after you say "*Goodbye*" roughly translates to "*Stay*" in some hidden language of the heart.

SPIRIT

Arouse My Curiosity

In my eyes, good conversation
is the birthplace of true attraction.
Open your heart
and share with me
every encounter and experience
that shaped you
into who you are today.
Tell me about
your hopes and dreams
and captivate me with your passions.
Arouse my curiosity
and you'll have my attention.

The Equation

Accept that not everyone
will understand you,
that every soul is its own equation.
While you may appear
as little more than
senseless gibberish to some,
others will need only a single look
to get a grasp of who you are.
Never dull,
dumb down,
or adjust yourself
to fit somewhere you don't belong.

Unique, Honest Self

The most important thing
you will ever do
in your life
is learn to embrace
your unique, honest self.
A boundless, infinitely populated universe
and there is nothing else here
quite like you.
This is your power.
All those things
that make you strange and different
also make you irreplaceable.

Self-Love

Self-love is an ocean and your heart
is a vessel. Make it full and any
excess will spill over into the lives
of the people you hold dear, but you
must come first.

Extremes

I am either guarded as a prison cell
or open as a wound. Always one
extreme or the other. You'll either
know nothing at all about me or
everything there is to know.

The Checklist

Happiness is not a checklist.
    A dream job,
    a fast car,
    a good home,
    even love,
mean nothing at all
if you have not yet found a way
to feel full and content
in your own mind and heart.

My Mantra

I am working
on learning
how to be whole and free
within myself,
to acknowledge
my brokenness,
manifest
my own happiness,
and succeed
and fail gracefully.

The Grand Canyon

She always taught me to admire my damage.
"Did you know," she would begin, *"that the Grand
Canyon was formed by the relentless current of the
Colorado River cutting into the earth over the course
of millions of years? See, even this world has scars,"*
she would say, *"and look how beautiful that can be."*

Opening Up

I rarely open up. I don't like to feel vulnerable or misunderstood. But now and again I get to talking to somebody, and something about them resonates with me. Whether total stranger or old friend, in their presence I feel a familiar calm wash over me, and everything comes gushing out.

Unresolved

In this life, you won't always find peace and closure. Some losses bury themselves into the heart too deeply to ever be entirely resolved or forgotten. Sometimes, the most you can really do is persevere until the pain is too small or familiar to harm you.

An Extraordinary Life

The difference between an ordinary life and an
extraordinary one is only a matter of perspective.
Pull the blinds. Look around you. It is a weird,
wonderful world and you do not require a
ten-digit bank account to immerse yourself in it.
Travel down dusty roads without a destination
in mind. Climb a mountain and scream out into the
void. Kiss a stranger. Skinny-dip in a lake. Get lost
and lose yourself—these are two separate things.
Explore the wilderness, particularly the one within.
Think less of destiny and more of the moment
right here. Because, in the end, as you reflect back
on your long life in that hospital bed, surrounded
by your family and friends, fame won't matter, nor
will the extent of your wealth. You are only the sum
of the stories you can tell.

Awfully Sentimental

I am awfully sentimental.
    Of books,
        belongings,
            people,
                places.
It matters very little how
positive or negative
the experience was.
If it shared some
meaningful time in my life,
I'll have trouble letting go.

Healthy Eating

Let loose once in a while. Stay up
too late, drink until you drop, order
the dirtiest, fattiest, most delicious
item on the menu.
  You cannot live your whole life
restricting yourself only to what
is good and healthy for the body.
Sometimes, you have to do what
is good and healthy for the soul.

Spiritual Connection

No one is too good for you. It all depends on the kind of attraction. You can be desired for your looks, status, or the size of your bank account, but when you are desired for you—your heart, your soul, the way your mind works—nothing else matters. Spiritual connection surpasses all else.

Displaced

The thing I can't stand most about myself is that
I'm so rarely settled. That I cannot allow myself
the space to feel satisfaction in what I have. That I
avoid intimacy at all costs and court difficult things.
That I dismantle everything I love because I am so
terrified of ends.

In Retrospect

If only you could recognize the beauty of a moment
before it left you. Memorize every minor detail so
you could relive precisely how it made you feel.
But sadly, the sweetest moments in life usually go
by unnoticed and rarely reveal their true weight
and worth until they are long behind you.

Black Coffee

I tend to be most interested in the kinds of people who do not sweeten or dilute themselves for the sake of people's tastes. Who never soften the blow of who they are. Like my coffee, I prefer the people I connect with to be full strength and searing hot. And able to rouse my weary, idle heart.

The Temple

Listen to me, your body is not a temple. Temples can be destroyed and desecrated. Your body is a forest. Thick canopies of maple trees and sweet-scented wildflowers sprouting in the underwood. You will grow back, over and over, no matter how badly you are devastated.

Unstoppable

She was unstoppable,
not because
she did not
have failures or doubts
but because
she continued on
despite them.

Night air,
good conversation,
and a sky full of stars
can heal almost
any wound.

Overcome

You aren't
what has happened to you,
    you are
how you've overcome it.

Wildflowers

Dear outsiders,
    even the most
    beautiful of wildflowers
    are considered
    weeds in the wrong gardens.

    What another
    thinks of you
    does not dictate your value.

Little Everyday Joys

I'm beginning to recognize that real happiness isn't
something large and looming on the horizon ahead
but something small, numerous, and already here.
A decent breakfast. A warm sunset. The smile
of someone you love. Your little everyday joys all
lined up in a row.

Get Over It

I cannot stand the words "*Get over it.*" All of us are under such pressure to put our problems into past tense.

Slow down. Don't allow others to hurry your healing. It is a process, one that may take years, occasionally even a lifetime, and that's okay.

Run Freely

Human beings
    are made of water.

We were not designed
    to hold ourselves
    together,

rather run freely
    like oceans,
    like rivers.

Courage

Softness
     is not
     weakness.

It takes
     courage
     to stay delicate

in a world
     this cruel.

Diamonds

On the difficult days,
when the world's
on your shoulders,

remember that diamonds
are made
under the weight
of mountains.

A Self-Destructive Heart

"My heart beats in almosts.
It's constantly in pursuit
of those whom it desires,
but the moment it comes too close,
it recoils,
trembles,
stops dead in its tracks,
and then bolts in the opposite direction.
I hold on to what makes me miserable
and I let the good things go.
I'm self-destructive," I said.
"It's the way I've always been."

"And why do you think that is?"

"Because it is easier
to destroy something you love,"
I replied,
"than it is to watch it leave."

Real Talk

If we're going to talk, then let's talk. Forget about
what is polite or proper and delve right into what
is sincere and honest. Lead me down through
the labyrinth of your true spectacular self.
I am not interested in pleasantries. If you want
a conversation, then let's get lost.

The Somber Air

Sad is something I can deal with when I'm aware
of its source. When I'm able to take time out to
develop a solution and work my way back to a
healthier state of mind.

    It's the not knowing that kills me. A vague
air of unhappiness I cannot understand, escape,
or destroy.

Full of Contrast

To me, a rich and satisfying life means one full
of contrast. Give me sleep-ins. And soft rains.
Coffee shops and conversation. But also adrenaline
and adventure. And drunken bellows to the stars.
I am determined to embrace this extravagant life
for all that it has to offer.

The Invitation

Please, do not mistake my tendency to be private and
standoffish for either sheepishness or arrogance.
Once you get to know me, you'll find I'm both lively
and kind.

These high walls aren't here because I want to
keep the whole world out. I'm just very particular
about who I invite back into mine.

You've Changed

"You've changed" is an insult often intended to discourage you. Ignore it. This is your growth. Adapting and refining yourself are all necessary parts of the process. So long as you continue to endeavor to be kind and compassionate you have nothing to be ashamed of.

The Yes-Man

I am learning to say *yes*, to be
daring and spontaneous, to hurl
myself into people and places
and moments without hesitation
or second-guessing myself, to
challenge my anxieties, to confront
my fears and trust unwaveringly in
chance and fate to lead me to where
I am supposed to be.

A memory
can be a
marvelous getaway,
but you must
never make
a home there.

A Healthy Heart

A gentle reminder
that your heart is a muscle
and so should be
exercised regularly.
Love often and love deeply.

The Dial

This heart of mine has
only two settings:
nothing at all or too much.
There is no in between.

Into Place

Chin up, child.
In my experience,
when a life
seems to be falling to pieces,
it is usually falling
into place.

Little Monsters

I'm afraid of opening up,
only I'm not sure
which frightens
me most,
letting you in
or the monsters out.

You Made It

I need you to pinpoint
the precise moment the idea of dying
became more beautiful to you
than how you feel in the mirror,
when your friends and family
began averting their eyes
and covering their ears
as though your tears were nails
screeching down a chalkboard,
when every inch of your being
first began kicking and screaming
at its own existence.
Now, dismantle it.
Tear it to pieces
and know that every breath
is a triumph, a victory,
and that each beat in your heart
is a clenched fist raised
to the world as its witness,
chanting, "*I made it, I made it, I made it.*"

The Path

What a terrible waste
of a life it is
to always take
the easy path,
to never know what it is
to risk everything for
what you love.

Rise & Shine

Rise and shine.
I've always
felt such fondness
for that sweet old phrase.
As though
we are all little suns.
As though
we are all someone's day.

The Hours

The hours between
12am and 6am
have a funny way
of making you feel
like you're either
on top of the world
or under it.

The Best Revenge

Truth is, the best revenge is seeking none at all and investing that energy in your own health and progress, prioritizing personal goals you've been neglecting, and working toward creating a passionate, prosperous, and fulfilling future of your own.

The Hourglass

It's strange how your childhood
sort of feels like forever,
then suddenly you're sixteen
and the world becomes an hourglass
and you're watching the sand
pile up at the wrong end.
And you're thinking of how, when
you were just a kid,
your heartbeat was like a kick drum
at a rock show,
and now it's just a time bomb
ticking out.
And it's sad.
And you want to forget about dying,
but mostly,
you just want to forget about
saying goodbye.

The Rebound

Listen, a rebound isn't the answer. The solution to a broken heart isn't finding something else to seal the wound but falling back in love with your solitary self.

It is relearning how to enjoy the company of your thoughts and trust in your capability to navigate a life on your own.

Sid & Nancy

I don't think I was built for a love that is comfortable or uncomplicated. There is a restlessness in me that will always be drawn to dark, madly passionate things. The intoxicating highs and devastating lows. The chaos and the conflict.

A Little Short

I am deathly afraid of almosts.
Of coming so very close
to where I want to be in life
that I can almost
touch it,
almost taste it,
then falling just a little short.

Whoever said
the small things
don't matter
has never seen
a match
start a wildfire.

Something Else

I cannot be still for long.
There is a riot in me all the time.
A needy, restless voice
in my heart
endlessly urging me onward.
I ache for new experiences
and my hunger
for adventure is boundless.
My entire life is a perpetual loop
of longing for something else.

My Walls

Say what you like.
I am not ashamed of my walls.
My boundaries are my own
and purposed for my shelter
while I am in healing and vulnerable.
I am regrouping.
Life can wait.
When I am good and ready
I will climb them.
Until then, let me be.

Little Brave

You are fierce.
You're a survivor.
You're a fighter
through and through.
Little brave,
breathe.
There is a warrior
within you.

Vacation

I need to move around a bit. To shuffle
my surroundings. To wake up in cities
I don't know my way around and have
conversations in languages I cannot
entirely comprehend.

There is always this tremendous
longing in my heart to be lost, to be
someplace else, to be far, far away
from all of this.

Loner at Heart

I am a loner at heart, though you wouldn't know it. I regularly make an effort to leave the house and mingle, and when I do I endeavor to appear both approachable and friendly.

However, in the back of my mind, there lies this dull, steady ache, begging me to leave.

The Enigma

I have a tendency to become infatuated with people who are distant and difficult to understand, who share themselves sparingly and rarely with their whole hearts.

I adore the mysteries and enigmas of people. The harder to solve, the better.

The Match

As of late I've found physical attraction is no longer enough. I need human connection. I need to undress the layers of a soul before I feel a desire to tear away any clothes. Passion remains the fire, but now intimacy strikes the match, and friendship has become the fuel.

Rain Clouds

It's going to be okay.
It might not feel like it right now,
but in time
all pain passes on.
In time
all rain clouds break for the sun.

The Climb

There will always be something else.
Another obstacle to overcome.
More danger on the horizon.
That is life.
But there's more to living
than conquering mountains
and coming out victorious
in every fight.
Enjoy the view.
Relax once in a while.
Your success is meaningless without joy.

About the Author

Beau Taplin is an internationally recognized author and social media sensation. Following a formative education at Melbourne Rudolf Steiner, Beau found some success as a songwriter before turning his passions to poetry and prose. He has been warmly embraced for his heartfelt, relatable content, which is now shared and read by millions worldwide. Beau's philosophy on life is simple: *make it meaningful.* Soon enough, we will all be bones in the ground, the oceans will dry up, the sun will burn out, and nobody will be around to remember we were here at all. So go, spend your time here with heart. Find what matters to you and manifest it while you can. Because while this universe we inhabit may be infinite and unfeeling, we are not, and that is our gift.

You can connect with Beau on Instagram and Twitter **@beautaplin** or on Facebook at **facebook.com/beauchristophertaplin**

You can also find a loving home for his other collections through his website at **beautaplin.com**